CONTENTS

INTRODUCTION

Seashells belong to one of the most varied groups of animals, the Mollusca. The name mollusc means 'soft-bodied' and their soft body is perhaps the only obvious characteristic which they all share. Most have a hard outer shell, some have an internal shell and others have no shell at all.

Although the six major groups or classes look quite distinct they share a common ancestry. The body-plan of one of the six classes, the *Monoplacophora*, is most likely that from which the others evolved. It is a primitive limpet-like creature with its head and mouth containing a ribbon-like 'tongue' embedded with numerous tiny 'teeth' known as the radula, at the front. Behind the head is a relatively large, flat-bottomed muscular foot and situated above the foot is the visceral mass containing a straight gut and paired internal organs. Surrounding the body and attached to the visceral mass is a thin envelope of tissue called the mantle. The space between it and the body is called the mantle cavity. This is the essential unifying feature of the molluscs.

The mantle defines the boundary between the environment and the internal organs in much the same way as skin does for the vertebrates. It is a relatively complex organ through which calcium carbonate is concentrated and secreted to form the shell.

The six principal classes of the phyllum Mollusca are usually listed in the following systematic order:
1 *Monoplacophora*
2 *Polyplacophora* (Chitons)
3 *Gastropoda* (Snails and Slugs)
4 *Scaphopoda* (Tusk shells)
5 *Bivalvia* (Clams, Mussels and Oysters)
6 *Cephalopoda* (Octopus, Squids and Nautilus)

Monoplacophora (Greek: single-plate bearing)

The simple cap-shaped, limpet-like shells of this class of molluscs have been found in rocks as old as the late Pre-Cambrian, some 570–600 million years ago. They probably evolved from a segmented ancestor.

Polyplacophora (Greek: many-plate bearing): Chitons

The Chitons are as ancient as the *Monoplacophora*. They form the sister-group of all other shelled molluscs. Their body-plan is primitive; they are bilaterally symmetrical with a broad, elongated foot.

Chitons are relatively small, the largest reaching little over 30cm (12 in).

Gastropoda (Greek: stomach-footed): Snails, slugs

The Gastropods are the largest and most varied of the classes with around 80,000 living species and probably as many extinct. Their origins can be traced back as far as the lower Cambrian (570 million years ago). They range in size from microscopic to 60cm (24 in) or more and have evolved from essentially marine animals to occupy freshwater, terrestrial and semi-arboreal habitats. There are both shelled (snails) and un-shelled (slugs) forms. Most snails have a coiled shell into which the animal may withdraw, closing the aperture with a 'trap door' (*operculum*) to limit the risk of drying out.

The body-plan of most snails is similar to that of Chitons with the fundamental difference of having a twisted gut.

Scaphopoda (Greek: boat-footed): Tusk shells

The Scaphopods form one of the smallest and most uniform groups of molluscs. They all have a simple hollow shell which resembles an

The Concise Illustrated Book of
Seashells

Solene Morris

GALLERY BOOKS
An imprint of W. H. Smith Publishers Inc.
112 Madison Avenue
New York, New York 10016

First published in the United States of America
by GALLERY BOOKS
An imprint of W.H. Smith Publishers Inc.
112 Madison Avenue
New York, New York 10016

ISBN 0–8317–1676–2

 Printed in Spain

Acknowledgments
All photographs supplied by Brian Trodd
Publishing House.
All artworks by Linden Artists with the
exception of the cover artworks by Maltings
Partnership

elephant's tusk. They are relatively small: the largest species may grow to no more than 13cm (5 in).

Scaphopods form a sister-group with the bivalves with whom they share a close common ancestry. However, they retain more features in common with the probable ancestor than do the bivalves.

Bivalvia (Latin: two-shelled): Clams, Mussels, Scallops, Oysters

The Bivalves are the second largest class with around 10,000 living species and possibly more fossils. Their ancestry, as sister-group of the Scaphopods, links the early bivalves through long extinct classes to the stem groups from which all molluscs evolved.

The body of most bivalves is laterally compressed and protected by two hard shells, hinged dorsally by interlocking 'teeth' and an elastic proteinaceous ligament set either externally or internally on the hinge plate. One or two adductor muscles hold the valves together.

Bivalves have no head or radula. The mouth is above the broad hatchet-shaped foot to the front of the visceral mass. The coiled gut opens posteriorly, waste products and spawn are ejected through an opening at the back of the mantle, which for many species is fused to form an exhalent siphon. Gills may be of several types; most assist feeding.

The sexes are separate in most species of bivalves and fertilization external. Free-swimming larvae may settle quickly or spend some time in the plankton before they metamorphose. Some species retain their larvae within the mantle cavity until they are sufficiently well developed.

Sunrise Tellin

Cephalopoda (Greek: head-footed): Octopus, Squids, Nautilus

The Cephalopods are the most highly specialized and most intelligent class of molluscs. They have an equally long history as the other major classes. There are around a thousand living species. The largest group is the octopuses with about 650 species: squids, with approximately 350 species form the next largest group. They are entirely marine and include the largest known mollusc: the Giant Squid which lives in the North Atlantic and can be over 20m (66 ft).

Most living cephalopods (octopuses and squids) have either no shell or an internal shell. Their body-plan is designed as a cylinder having a head with well-developed eyes at the front and eight arms. Squids also have two retractable tentacles which are used to capture their prey. At the back end the squids have a broad flange-like muscular tail fin which aids directional swimming. Octopuses and squids swim by ejecting strong jets of water from the forward, ventrally situated funnel. The mouth is located centrally between the arms and has a tough parrot-like beak used to bite and tear its prey which is then 'chewed' by the radula.

WEST INDIAN CHITON

Chiton tuberculosa

Linnaeus, 1758

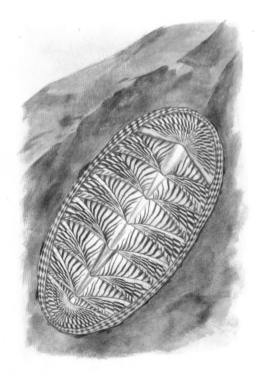

Common West Indian Chiton

Family: Chitonidae
Size: 8.5cm (3 in)
Habitat: Rocky shores, low intertidal zone, under stones in exposed areas
Distribution: Southern Florida to the West Indies
Description: The Common West Indian Chiton has a convex shell of eight separate overlapping plates or valves set in a wide, elliptical leathery girdle, sculptured with smooth, rounded scales. The two end valves are sculptured with numerous rows of beads radially arranged. The central six valves are partitioned into two broadly triangular lateral flanks with irregular bifurcating radial ridges and a smooth median area.

The colour of the shell is uniformly grey to brown or flecked with darker spots. The ribs are a lighter shade or white. The girdle is patterned with alternating light and dark patches of the same colour as the shelly valves.

They live on rocks from the low intertidal zone to depths of around 180m (600 ft). Chitons usually forage at night, rasping algae from the surface of the rocks, returning to rest under rocks, in crevices and beneath overhanging ledges where they clamp very tightly to the surface.

Reproduction is carried out by external fertilization from separate sexes. The eggs may be produced in a gelatinous mass or develop directly in the plankton.

There are several hundred species of chitons found worldwide from the Arctic to the tropics.

Family: Haliotidae
Habitat: Rocky shores in the sublittoral zone; commonly occurring at depths between 6–20m (20–65 ft)
Size: 20–30cm (8–12 in)
Distribution: Pacific Coast of North America, from Washington State to southern California
Importance: Commercially fished as valuable edible species; shells prized for use as ornaments and in jewellery
Description: The Red Abalone is one of the largest species of the genus *Haliotis* with a maximum size of about 30cm (1 ft). The colour of the shell is rust to brick-red. The surface is sculptured with 4 to 5 irregular wavy ribs often interrupted by growth lines. The holes are slightly raised with only the last 3 or 4 open. The pearly interior of the shell is iridescent pink to light bluish-green with a large central muscle scar.

The Abalone is an openly coiled shell, characterized by a curved row of open holes which allow for the ejection of waste products and spawn. The shell surface may be eroded by small boring or encrusting organisms.

Abalones feed by grazing the rock surface primarily for algae. They, in turn, are not only a delicacy for human consumption, but are an important part of the diet of the other animals such as the Giant Pacific Octopus and the Sea Otter.

Overfishing has reduced the numbers of Red Abalone and conservation measures have been imposed by some states. The oil spill in the northern part of their range in 1989 will almost certainly mean the virtual extinction of a major section of the population of this species in that region of the world.

Red Abalone

ATLANTIC OYSTER DRILL

Urosalpinx cinerea

Say, 1822

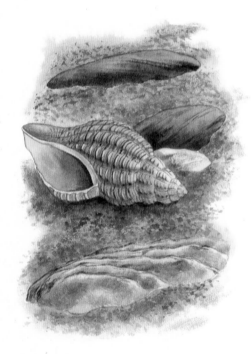

Atlantic Oyster Drill

Family: Muricidae
Size: 2.5cm (1 in)
Habitat: On coarse pebbles and shell debris, among oyster beds, sublittoral zone to about 8m (26 ft)
Distribution: North Atlantic from Nova Scotia to Florida; introduced into northern Europe and the Pacific Northwest from Washington to California
Importance: A major predator of the American Oyster and native oysters where accidentally introduced with the American (Eastern) species
Description: The Atlantic Oyster Drill is a small, solid, elongated shell with 7 whorls at an acute apical angle (40°). It is sculptured by 12 low axial ribs which are crossed by coarse spiral cords and finer cords in between the ribs. The colour is ash-grey to dull white or pale brownish-orange with darker bands. The aperture is oval with a short but distinct anterior siphonal canal. The inner margin of the outer lip is rarely thickened, and defined by up to six small teeth.

This species is a major pest among oyster beds. It feeds on the oysters, drilling into the shell by use of the radula and chemical secreted from its accessory boring organ in much the same way as the Moon Snail. The holes drilled by this species are straight-sided.

During the late spring the animals move up into the low intertidal zone to spawn. Females produce 25–30 goblet-shaped egg capsules in which 8–12 eggs are laid. They are attached singly to rocks or shells. Development takes place entirely within the capsule. Within a couple of months the young snails emerge at the crawling stage.

BASKET WHELK

Nassarius fossatus

(Gould, 1849)

Family: Nassariidae
Size: 5cm (2 in)
Habitat: Sandy shores, on sand and mud from low intertidal zone to around 18m (60 ft)
Distribution: Pacific coast of North America from British Columbia to Baja California
Description: A fairly large solid shell, it is conical, having 8 or 9 modestly convex whorls. The body whorl is only modestly expanded.

The shell is evenly coloured creamy beige to orange. It is sculptured by 6–7 spiral cords crossed by numerous curved axial ribs giving a more or less uniformly beaded appearance. The oval aperture is pointed towards the narrow posterior notch and opens to the short, broad anterior siphonal canal. The rim of the outer lip has numerous low rounded ridge-like teeth.

The Basket Whelks form a large family of around 350 species. They may be found in very large populations, living beneath the surface, from just below the low tide level to depths of around 18m (60 ft).

Most species of Basket Whelk are scavengers, emerging from the sand in large numbers when they sense the presence of a potential source of food. Many species are also predators. One species feeds on the egg-masses of polychaete worms; others feed on the egg capsules of other molluscs.

The Giant Western Basket Whelk has been reported to feed on small bivalves. The sexes are separate and shells of the females may be somewhat larger than the males. Numerous eggs are laid in distinctive pouch-like egg capsules which may be fixed singly to seaweeds or grasses.

Great Western Basket Whelk

11

BLADDER BUBBLE SHELL

Hydatina vesicaria

(Lightfoot, 1786)

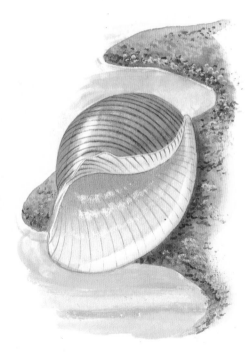

Bladder Bubble Shell

Family: Hydatinidae
Size: 4.5cm (1¾ in)
Habitat: Sandy shores, in the sublittoral zone, burrowing in fine sand or swimming in shallow water
Distribution: Southern Florida, the West Indies to Brazil
Description: This is also known as the Brown-lined Paper Bubble Shell. The shell is thin and fragile, ovate or globular in shape with the initial whorls completely enveloped by the inflated body whorl. The aperture is a wide pear-shaped opening with a thin, smooth outer lip that narrows towards the top.

The shell may be creamy white to tan, spirally patterned by numerous brown to black, slightly wavy lines. The body of the animal is rusty brown to orange, outlined around its entire body and mantle flap with a narrow border of pale blue.

Bubble Shells form a small but widespread family with around a dozen species living mainly in shallow tropical seas.

They have fairly large bodies characterized by an extensive mantle flap (parapodium) which is used in an undulating wave-like motion to allow the animal to swim gracefully. It has no operculum – however, it is able to withdraw completely into the shell. The animal shelters by burrowing in fine sand.

Most species are predators, feeding on polychaete worms. Bladder Bubble Shells migrate into more shallow water in order to spawn. They are hermaphrodites, producing several thousand eggs in long gelatinous ribbons which may be attached to weeds or hard objects. The larvae hatch as free-swimming veligers.

Family: Strombidae
Size: 30cm (12 in)
Habitat: Sandy shores, subtidally in sand, among eelgrass to depths of around 5m (16 ft)
Distribution: Bermuda, southeastern Florida and the West Indies; Venezuela to Brazil
Importance: Used in Conch Chowder and other popular dishes in Florida and the West Indies. Shells are also prized collectors' items.

Description: The large, thick, heavy shell, up to about 30cm (12 in) in height, is characterized, when adult, by a distinctive broad flaring lip to the aperture which is usually pink with a pearly lustre. The upper edge of the apertural lip may extend above the apex of the spire. The general colour of the shell is yellowish white with streaks of tan, covered when alive with a thin brown periostracum which readily flakes away when dry. The spire is tall with 5 or 6 whorls distinguished by relatively sharp pointed knobs. Those of the body-whorl are quite prominent. Young specimens lack the large expanded lip but have distinctive sharply angled whorls with about 8 knobs on each.

Most species of conches are able to move quite rapidly by using the pointed operculum on the back of their foot. When dug into wet sand the shell can be pushed up and over allowing the animal to jump clear of potential predators.

The females produce eggs in long gelatinous tubes from which the larvae hatch as free-swimming veligers.

Shells and meat of the Queen Conch are highly prized and as a result of over-collecting they may become an endangered species.

Queen Conch

CROWN CONE

Conus regius

Gmelin, 1791

Crown Conch

Family: Conidae
Size: 7.6cm (3 in)
Habitat: On reefs, under rocks and among rubble, sublittoral zone to a depth of about 5m (15 ft)
Distribution: Southern Florida, the West Indies to Brazil
Description: The shape of the shell is generally conical; the short spire forms an acute angle above the flattened penultimate whorl. The outer apertural lip is nearly straight and the opposite side of the body whorl tapers from the slightly convex shoulder to the narrow, open, anterior siphonal canal. There is a row of small rounded knobs above the sutures of the spiral whorls and larger, more prominent knobs around the shoulder of the body whorl. The apical whorls are sculptured by fine spiral cords crossed by axial lines to give a fine beaded texture.

Cone Shells are predators, hunting mainly at night. Sand dwelling species lie in wait below the surface with their siphon projecting, detecting their prey by means of a chemical receptor organ. When the prey is within striking distance the Cone quickly emerges and ejects its harpoon-like radula tooth into the victim, stunning it with a poisonous venom. The venom is produced in the poison gland and passed along the coiled poison duct to a chamber near where the radular teeth are stored. After the tooth has been used another is transferred from the radular sac where it was produced. The poison is a neurotoxin and that of a few species is sufficiently potent to kill humans.

Family: Neritidae
Size: 0.5cm (¼ in)
Habitat: Exposed rocky shores, in the intertidal zone to a depth of around 7m (20 ft)
Distribution: Caribbean, rare in southern Florida; the Mediterranean
Description: A small glossy shell of bright green colour, the Emerald Nerite is marked with white dots and streaks radiating from the apical whorls on to the broadly expanded

Smaragdia viridis

(Linnaeus, 1758)

body whorl. Both the shell and body are green.

The Nerites are compact, low spired, thick-shelled snails which live attached to rocks in the intertidal zone on exposed rocky shores. The shells may be either sculptured with coarse to fine radial ribs or smooth with either a dull or glossy surface. There are several hundred marine species and a number of brackish and freshwater species. The majority of species are found in the tropics and warm temperate regions. However, the northernmost representative of this group is the freshwater Nerite *Theodoxus fluviatilis* (Linnaeus), which lives in chalky rivers and canals in Britain and northern Europe.

The sexes are separate and fertilization is internal. The female produces numerous dome-shaped proteinaceous egg capsules in which several eggs may be deposited. The capsules are attached singly to the rock surface. Development takes place entirely within the capsules.

Nerites are probably all algal grazers, feeding on the algal covering of the rocks upon which they live. They are found in fairly large populations. Their variety has made them popular with collectors.

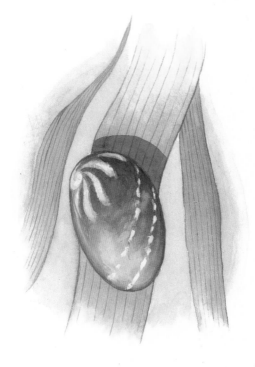

Emerald Nerite

HORN SHELL

Cerithium eburneum

Bruguiere, 1792

Ivory Horn Shell

Family: Cerithiidae
Size: 2.5cm (1 in)
Habitat: Sandy shores, shallow sublittoral zone; reef-flats with sand and sea grass
Distribution: Southeastern Florida, Bahamas and the West Indies
Description: The Ivory Horn Shell has an elongated spiral shell with sharply angled apex (35°). There are 10–12 whorls sculptured with 4–7 spiral rows of beads. The beads in the central row of each whorl tend to be slightly larger. The whorls are also distinguished by several fairly prominent axial varices. The colour of the shell is cream or ivory with brown to reddish-brown blotches which sometimes merge to give a more generally brownish colour. The varices (or axial ribs) usually remain white. The outer lip of the aperture is reflexed and wavy where the spiral cords end and occasionally thickened when a varix is produced. The siphonal notch is short.

The scientific name of this family of shells is derived from the Greek word *keration* meaning 'little horn'. The species described, *eburneum*, comes from a Latin word which means 'made of ivory'.

The Horn Shells are common on shallow tropical and subtropical shores living in fairly large populations in sand and among sea grasses. This is a large family with 14 or more genera and around 30 species in North America. Free-swimming larvae emerge from gelatinous egg masses laid by the females among turtle grass. The Ivory Horn Shell feeds on algae which it grazes from the turtle grass, a variety of sea grass.

KING HELMET

Cassis tuberosa

Linnaeus, 1758

Family: Cassididae
Size: 23cm (9 in)
Habitat: Sandy shores from the sub-littoral zone to depths of around 20m (60 ft)
Distribution: North Carolina to Brazil; common in the West Indies
Description: A moderately large, heavy shell with the body whorl greatly expanded. It is distinctly sculptured by a fine reticulate pattern, spirally crossed by three rows of blunt, triangular-shaped knobs which decrease in size toward the reflexed anterior siphonal canal. The ventral side is covered by a thick triangular shield, characteristic of this genus. The aperture is elongated and relatively narrow, with 11 blunt, ridge-like, white teeth along the inner margin of the outer lip. The colour of the shield is beige to creamy pink. The dorsal surface of the shell is yellowish to pinkish brown marked by darker chevron-shaped streaks, occasionally in bands around the body whorl. The outer lip is marked by 4 or 5 distinct dark spots.

Helmet Shells live mainly in sand or gravel where they hunt and feed upon sea-urchins, sand-dollars and other echinoids. They crawl over and immobilize their prey with their large, powerful foot.

The shells of most species are prized by collectors for their decorative value. For centuries craftsmen have exploited the different coloured shell layers in the carving of cameos. The typical cameo is carved in a white outer layer with the underlying coral pink layer exposed. This is one of three species found on the southeastern (or eastern) coast of the U.S.

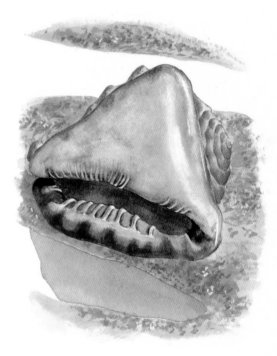

King Helmet

LIGHTNING WHELK

Busycon contrarium

(Conrad, 1864)

Lightning Whelk

Family: Melongenidae
Size: 45cm (18 in)
Habitat: Sandy shores, from low intertidal zone to about 3m (10 ft)
Distribution: North Carolina to Florida; Texas (Gulf of Mexico)
Description: The shell is sinistrally (left-hand) coiled with a low conical spire of about 4 whorls and an inflated body whorl with a broad aperture tapering to a long narrow siphonal canal. The whorls are distinctly angled above the sutures. A single row of 16–18 blunt, triangular knobs encircles the shell at the shoulder of the body whorl. The colour is grey to creamy white with dark axial stripes coincident with the knobs.

There are only a few species of this genus. They occur only on the Atlantic and Gulf coasts of North America. They feed on bivalves, mainly hard-shelled clams which the snail traps beneath the sand and opens by forcing the valves apart with its strong muscular foot.

The females produce long strings of leathery disc-like egg capsules which are between 1.2–2cm (½–¾ in) in diameter and about 0.6cm (¼ in) wide, with a distinctly ribbed circumference. Numerous eggs are laid in each capsule where they develop to the crawling stage before emerging.

One species, the Channeled Whelk *Busycon canaliculatum* (Linnaeus, 1758), was sold until early this century for food in Boston, Massachusetts.

The Fulgur Whelks have been traditionally classified with the Crown Conches to which they may not be as closely related as was previously considered.

Patella vulgata

Linnaeus, 1758

Family: Patelleidae
Size: 7.5cm (3 in)
Habitat: Rocky shores from the high intertidal to shallow sublittoral zones
Distribution: Eastern Atlantic, from Scandinavia to the Mediterranean
Importance: Gathered for food since pre-historic times, particularly in Europe
Description: Limpets are characterized by a simple, modestly thick, conical shell that may be smooth or coarsely ribbed. The Common Limpet is usually dark grey or brown in colour with mottled darker bands that may be coincident with the growth increments. The shape of the shell seems to be controlled to some extent by the position occupied on the shore.

The body-plan of the limpets is very similar to that of the abalones. The head, bearing sensory organs, and very large broad foot are protected by clamping the shell down tightly on to the rock surface. Repeated attachment to the same place produces an indentation in the rock surface. Limpets are algal grazers, seldom wandering far from their 'home scar'; they return after feeding and at low tide.

The Common Limpet spawns in late autumn, fertilization is external and larvae are planktotrophic, feeding initially on microscopic plants before settling below the low tide level. As the young limpet develops it gradually migrates up the shore until it finds a suitable home. Once settled, limpets rarely stray more than a few metres.

Limpets are found on rocky shores throughout the world from cold temperate regions to the warmest tropical seas.

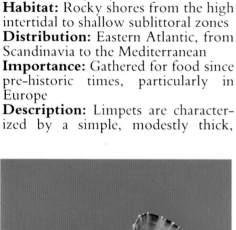

Slipper Limpet

MOON SNAIL

Natica catena

(da Costa, 1778)

Necklet Moon Snail

Family: Naticidae
Size: 3.5cm (1½ in)
Habitat: Sandy shores, low intertidal zone to around 200 m (650 ft), burrowing in sand
Distribution: Northwest Europe, from Britain to the Mediterranean
Description: This is also known as the Necklace Shell. It has a globose shell with a short spire of 4 or 5 whorls. The adult shell has 7 whorls: the last, body whorl is greatly expanded. The surface is smooth, lined only by the fine growth increments. The general shell colour is pale beige to creamy white, marked by a broken band of tan to brownish patches near the top of each whorl near the suture. The aperture is roughly semicircular with the inner lip distinguished by a thickened white callus and large, open umbilicus.

The Moon Snails belong to a large family of several hundred species distributed throughout the world. Virtually all the species are active predators, feeding mainly upon other molluscs, principally bivalves that they are able to catch below the surface of the sand in which they live. They feed by drilling a steep-sided hole through the shell of their prey, using their radula to scrape away shell material dissolved by a chemical secreted by an accessory boring organ.

Each species of Moon Snail produces its own distinctive egg masses in a generally broad gelatinous ribbon covered by fine sand. The Necklet Moon Snail produces a single incomplete circle, giving rise to the popular name 'sand collar'.

Janthina janthina

(Linnaeus, 1758)

Family: Janthinidae
Size: 2.5cm (1 in)
Habitat: Open ocean, floating on rafts of mucous bubbles. Associated with jellyfish
Distribution: Worldwide, found in subtropical and tropical regions. In the Atlantic along the Gulf Stream occasionally drifting as far north as New England on the North American coast and southwestern England (Cornwall)

Description: The Violet Sea Snails form a small snail family of only two genera with no more than eight species. They live in the open ocean, floating upside-down, supported by a raft of bubbles formed by a sticky mucous secretion produced by a gland in the front end of the foot which hardens in sea water. They are commonly found associated with jellyfish such as the Portuguese Man-of-War (*Physalia physalis*) and the By-The-Wind-Sailor (*Velella velella*) upon which they feed. The colour pattern of the shell helps to camouflage the snails from potential predators. From below, the lighter coloured dorsal side (top of the shell) is seen against the bright surface of the water, and from above the darker base blends with the purple tentacles of the jellyfish.

Violet Sea Snails change sex as they mature. They develop initially as males, changing later to females. Some species attach their egg capsules to the underside of their bubble raft where they hatch. However, the larvae of the Common Violet Sea Snail are released directly into the plankton as free-swimming veligers.

Violet Sea Snails occur in very large numbers and are commonly washed ashore after storms.

Violet Sea Snail

SLIPPER LIMPET

Crepidula fornicata

(Linnaeus, 1758)

Slipper Limpet

Family: Crepidulidae
Size: 6.5cm (2½ in)
Habitat: Rocky shores, on rock or other shells, from the intertidal zone to about 18m (50 ft)
Distribution: North Atlantic, Canada to Florida and the Gulf of Mexico, introduced into Britain and northwestern Europe and the Pacific Northwest (Puget Sound)
Importance: It causes damage as a fouling organism, particularly on oyster beds
Description: This limpet is also known as the Vaulted Slipper Limpet. This species has a modestly sized cap-shaped shell with a pointed apex at one end, curved and convexly arched to produce a widely expanded body whorl which has the appearance of a limpet. The shells of slipper limpets are distinguished from true limpets by the presence of a shelf-like septum which covers about half the width of the aperture.

The colour of the shell is dull creamy-white, streaked with light reddish-brown to pink in an irregular pattern radiating from the curved apex to the wide margin.

The Common or Vaulted Slipper Limpet begins life as a male, gradually passing through a true hermaphrodite phase before finally developing into a mature female. Females produce egg capsules which may contain up to 100 eggs. The capsules are attached to hard surfaces such as rocks or oyster shells where they are brooded until the free swimming larvae hatch.

Slipper Limpets need not move far from the place where they first settle because they feed by filtering microscopic particles from seawater.

Architectonica nobilis

Röding, 1798

Family: Architectonicidae
Size: 6.5cm (2½in)
Habitat: Sandy shores, below the surface in the sublittoral zone
Distribution: Atlantic and Pacific coasts of North America, from North Carolina to the Gulf of Mexico in the east, and from Mexico to Peru in the west
Description: Almost perfectly circular in outline, the Noble Sundial has a moderately low conical spire. Its

sculpture is of spiral cords, beaded on the apical whorls and flattened and indistinct on the body whorl. The base of the shell is characterized by a deep umbilicus, the rim of which is heavily beaded. The shell colour is creamy-yellow with a row of reddish-brown spots below the sutures and lighter spots on the spiral cords. The shell aperture is closed by a thin, brown corneous operculum characterized by lamellate growth lines.

The Sundials are a fairly uniform group of marine snails of which this species is one of the largest. Virtually all the species have similar shells. Members of the family are found in warm temperate and tropical regions around the world, and are often associated with pennatulids (Sea Pansies).

They develop from free swimming veligers which remain in the plankton as tiny left-hand (sinistral) coiled larvae. They continue to coil sinistrally, back over the apex of the larval shell, to become right-hand (dextral) coiled shells on settling, continuing to develop into dextrally coiled adults.

Their feeding behaviour is not well known, but some species are reported to feed at night, upside-down, on sponges.

Noble Sundial

TOP SHELL

Calliostoma zizyphinum

(Linnaeus, 1758)

Family: Trochidae
Size: 3.5cm (1.5 in)
Habitat: Rocky shores, in the low intertidal to sublittoral zones
Distribution: Britain and northwestern Europe
Description: The Painted Top Shell is broadly pyramidal in outline, with a flattened base. The diameter and height are approximately equal, sides diverging at an angle of about 75°. There are 10–12 whorls sculptured with slightly raised coils. The colour varies from creamy yellow or pale pink marked with streaks of darker shades of orange to reddish-brown, often flecked with white.

This is the prettiest of the top shells found in northwestern Europe and possibly the most variable in colour, ranging from purple to nearly white, but it is unmistakable in its distinctive 'top' shape.

The Painted Top Shell lives below the low tide level on rocks where it feeds by grazing among seaweeds and sponges. The sexes are separate in this species and the eggs are tiny and yellow, looking like mustard seeds. Hundreds of eggs are produced in a long gelatinous ribbon. The larvae develop within the egg-ribbon, emerging as tiny crawling snails.

There are several species of *Calliostoma* top shells in the western Atlantic, Caribbean and Pacific coastal regions of the Western Hemisphere. These species are similar to the European species in size, shape and general colour markings, though usually none is as beautifully coloured.

Painted Top Shell

Trivia monacha

(da Costa, 1778)

Family: Triviidae
Size: 1.5cm (½ in)
Habitat: Rocky shore from low intertidal zone to a depth of a few metres, under stones associated with sea-squirts (ascidians)
Distribution: Britain and the Atlantic coast of France, south to the Mediterranean
Description: The shell is small, brownish-pink dorsally to creamy-white ventrally; moderately thick, rounded 'coffee-bean' shaped. It is characterized by about 20 low ribs crossing the surface horizontally and branching towards the ventral, apertural side. A pale pink or whitish streak runs longitudinally along the arched dorsal surface, marking the line of extension of the mantle. Two or three darker, brownish blotches may also occur on the back. The aperture is narrow and curved towards both ends of the shell, edged by 'teeth' formed by the ribs which virtually encircle the shell. The body colour of the animal is usually reddish-orange.

The spire of the juvenile shell is overgrown as the animal grows to produce the characteristic domed shape typical of most cowries. The true cowries (genus *Cypraea*) are generally much larger and have smooth, very glossy shells.

Trivia species live on small sea-squirts. They penetrate the colonies with their extended proboscis, at the end of which is the mouth with rasp-like radula. The extended siphon allows the animal to draw in currents which supply oxygen-rich water for respiration. Egg capsules are vase-shaped and are laid within cavities excavated in the ascidian colonies.

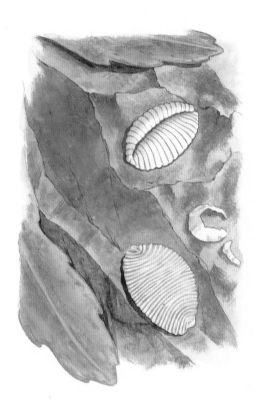

Trivia or Coffee Bean Cowrie

TUN SHELL

Tonna galea

(Linnaeus, 1758)

Giant Tun Shell

Family: Tonnidae
Size: 17.8cm (7 in)
Habitat: Off-shore, subtidally on sandy bottoms to a depth of around 13m (40 ft)
Distribution: North Carolina to Florida and the Gulf of Mexico; also the Mediterranean and West Africa
Description: A globose, relatively thin-shelled species characterized by a low conical spire of about 3–4 whorls expanding to a greatly inflated body whorl and a wide semi-circular aperture. The colour is typically a uniform creamy-beige to cocoa-brown, but occasionally the colour is broken into an irregular mottled pattern. The surface is sculptured with 18–21 low rounded spiral ribs. The aperture lip is thin and regularly waved, reflecting the position of the ribs. There is a short, open siphonal canal.

Tun Shells form a relatively small family of about 20 species. Most have large globose spirally ribbed thin shells. They live buried in sand subtidally to moderate depths in warm subtropical and tropical seas. They have a large muscular foot with no operculum.

The mouth is at the end of a long proboscis which may be greatly expanded to engulf whole the sea-cucumbers (holothurians) upon which they feed.

The eggs are laid by the females in broad ribbons arranged in rows. The larvae hatch as free-swimming veligers and remain in the plankton for several months prior to settling. Their long larval stage allows for the virtually worldwide dispersal of this species by ocean currents.

Epitonium indianorum

(Carpenter, 1864)

Family: Epitoniidae
Size: 2.5cm (1 in)
Habitat: Rocky to gravelly shores, sublittorally to depths of around 30m (100 ft)
Distribution: From Alaska to Vancouver Island in the shallow sublittoral zone, and to Southern California in deeper water of around 30m (100 ft)
Description: This is also known as the Spiral Staircase Shell. Its shell is white, elongated with 8–9 whorls distinguished by 13 or 14 raised and slightly recurved axial ribs on each whorl. The sutures between the whorls are well defined, and the ribs may be distinctly pointed at the shoulder. The aperture is oval with a slightly thickened lip.

Wentletraps are generally elongated shells, uniformly coloured. Most of the 200 or more species are white, cream or brownish in colour. The sculpture of virtually all species is prominent axial ribs which vary in thickness, angle and sharpness. Most species live in deep water. However, there are several species which may be found in the shallow sublittoral zone where they live in sand among rocks and gravel. Some species feed on sea anemones. They secrete a fluid which may act to anaesthetize the anemone when feeding.

Females lay their egg capsules in sand which covers the sticky surface before the capsules dry. Numerous egg capsules may be clustered, connected by a thread of string of the same flexible material. The larvae hatch as free-swimming veligers.

The name 'Indian Money Wentletrap' is derived from the ancient use of this species as a medium of exchange between American Indian tribes.

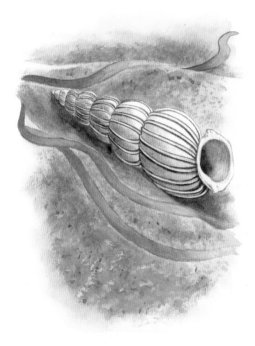

Indian Money Wentletrap

WHELK

Buccinum undatum

Linnaeus, 1758

Common Whelk

Family: Buccinidae
Size: 12.7cm (5 in)
Habitat: Rocky shores, low intertidal zone to about 60m (200 ft) on coarse sand and gravel
Distribution: North Atlantic from the Arctic to New Jersey; and northern Europe
Importance: In Europe, particularly in Britain and France, the Common Whelk or Bulot is sold either cooked and pickled or live
Description: A moderately large dull chalky white to tan shell, covered with traces of a thin, brownish periostracum. The shell is slightly elongated with 7–8 whorls of which the body whorl is the most inflated. It has 18–20 low curved undulating axial ribs crossed by around 16 strong cords, and finer cords in between and towards the anterior siphonal canal. The aperture is broadly oval with the outer lip slightly flared.

The Common Whelk is one of over 1,500 species of Buccinids. They are found from the cold Arctic and Antarctic seas to the tropics and from the intertidal zone to depths well over 500m (16,000 ft). The cold water species are usually thin to moderately thick shelled, while the species which live in the tropics are generally smaller with thicker shells. Many whelks are active predators, feeding on a variety of other marine organisms, mainly polychaete worms.

The sexes are separate in the Common Whelk and spawning takes place subtidally in early spring. The female produces a ball of fibrous egg capsules, each usually containing few eggs, only one of which normally hatches at the crawling stage.

Whelks are fished commercially off the east coast of England and the Atlantic coast of France.

Littorina littorea

(Linnaeus, 1758)

Family: Littorinidae
Size: 3.5cm (1½ in)
Habitat: Rocky shores, among gravel in the intertidal and sublittoral zones
Distribution: North Atlantic, North America from Canada to Maryland; Northwestern Europe from northern Norway to the Mediterranean
Importance: Valued as an edible species and for decorative ornaments since prehistoric times in Europe
Description: The shell of the Common Winkle, which is also known as

the Periwinkle, is fairly thick, conical with a modest spire of 4–5 whorls above the widest body whorl. The apex forms an angle of about 75°. The surface is covered by numerous fine spiral bands which are often darker than the ground colour of the shell which may be grey, brown or nearly black. The inner lip of the aperture is usually white with a dark margin.

Winkles or Periwinkles are widely distributed throughout the world from the cold temperate to tropical regions. They occupy an equally wide variety of habitats from the typical rocky shores among seaweeds to the trunks, and sometimes leaves, of mangrove trees. Most species feed on microscopic algae grazed from the surface of rocks or seaweeds. They forage mainly during the high tides, sheltering in crevices and among weeds at low tide.

The sexes are separate in the Common Winkle. The female produces floating disc-shaped capsules in which several eggs develop until the capsule dissolves releasing the free-swimming veliger larvae. The larvae continue their development in the sea, floating in and out with the changing tides until finally settling on the rocky shore.

Common Winkle

INDIAN MONEY TUSK SHELL

Dentalium pretiosum

Sowerby, 1860

Indian Money Tusk Shell

Family: Dentaliidae
Size: 5cm (2 in)
Habitat: Sandy shores, sublittoral zone to around 160m (525 ft); burrowing in sand and silty mud
Distribution: Pacific coast of North America from Alaska to southern California
Description: The shell is slightly curved, stout, tubular and white to creamy yellow in colour. It expands gradually from the narrow apex (posterior end) towards the front, which is twice as wide. The apex is distinguished by a moderately deep slit-like notch. The top is usually eroded. The shell surface is virtually smooth, sculptured only by the fine transverse growth lines.

Tusk Shells are distributed worldwide, living in the sublittoral zone to deep water. They live beneath the surface, burrowing through the sediment by expanding their elongated foot and protruding it downwards and then contracting it to effectively drag the curved shell forwards.

Clean water is drawn in through the opening at the top and waste products and gametes discharged. Fertilization is external; larvae develop in the plankton prior to settling.

Tusk Shells are active predators, feeding by capturing small animals such as foraminifera (small shelled protozoans) and tiny bivalves which also live in sand. The animal does not have a head, but has a number of fine extensible thread-like captaculae with which it seizes its prey.

The Indian Money Tusk Shell was used as a medium of exchange ('wampum') by the Nootka Indians of the Pacific Northwest (Vancouver Island, British Columbia).

Arca zebra

Swainson, 1833

Family: Arcidae
Size: 9cm (3½ in)
Habitat: Rocky shores and coral reefs from low intertidal zone to depths of around 6m (20 ft), attached to rock
Distribution: North Carolina, Bermuda to the West Indies and Brazil
Description: The Turkey Wing Ark is also known as the Zebra Ark – hence its Latin name. The shell is subrectangular in outline, higher at the truncated posterior end than the rounded anterior end. The umbones are closer to the front end by one quarter of the shell length. The shell is inflated with a wide flat interumbonal area and a straight hinge line. It is lined by the distinctive chevron pattern of the ligament. The mid-shell region is weakly depressed. About 35 low, rounded ribs radiate from the beaks crossed by finer growth lines. The colour is creamy to yellowish white with dark reddish-brown lines in the pattern of a V or wide W, centred on the umbones, increasing in size and width ventrally such that only the outer limbs remain as oblique stripes.

The hinge line is straight and has numerous even comb-like teeth. The interior shell is distinguished by two large, subequal adductor muscle scars. They are joined ventrally by a distinct pallial line which is indented only slightly where it meets the posterior adductor scar. When the two valves are closed the ventral line gapes in the mid-shell region to accommodate the thick byssus by which the animal is attached to the substrate.

Ark Shells have a worldwide distribution and may be found intertidally to great depths from the cold temperate regions to the tropics.

Turkey Wing or Ark Shell

31

BLUE MUSSEL

Mytilus edulis

Linnaeus, 1758

Edible or Blue Mussel

Family: Mytilidae
Size: 7.5cm (3 in)
Habitat: Rocky shores, low intertidal to sublittoral zones, attached to rocks or other hard substrates
Distribution: Worldwide, probably native to the North Atlantic from the Arctic to South Carolina in the west and Western Europe in the east; introduced to the Pacific coast and elsewhere
Importance: A popular and abundant food species utilized since prehistoric times
Description: Also known as the Edible Mussel, this moderately inflated shell is bluntly pointed at the front end and broadly rounded posteriorly. The beaks are at the front end of the shell. The colour ranges from yellowish-amber with darker brown to purple rays (mainly in young specimens), to the more typical shades of blue and violet to nearly black. The periostracum is thin and usually black. The inflated umbonal region is often eroded revealing the whiter shell layer below. The surface is smooth, sculptured only by the growth lines. The inside of the shell is often pearly in appearance and usually a slightly lighter shade of bluish-purple with the muscle scars darker and distinct.

The pallial line is not indented; it connects the large posterior adductor scar with the tiny, virtually obsolete anterior scar. The hinge line is curved and has only a very few small ridge-like teeth just below the beaks.

The Edible or Blue Mussel has long been an important source of food. This species occurs in vast populations in shallow water, attached to hard substrates by thin but strong byssal threads.

Cerastoderma edule

(Linnaeus, 1758)

Family: Cardiidae
Size: 5cm (2 in)
Habitat: Sandy shores, intertidal to sublittoral zones, burrowing to depth not greater than size of shell, in muddy sand to coarse gravel
Distribution: Northern Europe from the Baltic to the Mediterranean
Importance: A valuable food species, particularly in Britain where it is gathered commercially in many areas mainly on the east coast

Description: A small, solid, creamy white, globose shell characterized by about 25 closely-spaced radial ribs which are slightly flattened and crossed by raised thread-like growth lines to give a slightly scaly texture. The scales are stronger on the anterior and posterior slopes than the mid-shell area. The surface is covered by a thick brown periostracum which is usually eroded from all but the ventral and posterior margins. The external ligament is large and distinct.

The inside of the shell is white with the muscle scars indistinct. They are subequal, situated just below the ends of the hinge line and joined by an unbroken pallial line. The hinge is curved with two laterals either side of the small peg-like cardinal teeth in the right valve with corresponding sockets in the left valve.

A large worldwide family of nearly 200 species, the Cockles live from the shallow intertidal zone to great depths. Cockles are active burrowers using their muscular blade-like foot to dig rapidly into the sand or push against firm sand to jump away from predators. Oyster Catchers and Gulls, as well as crabs and snails such as the Whelk, are common enemies of the Edible Cockle.

Edible Cockle

DATE MUSSEL

Lithophaga antillarum

(d'Orbigny, 1842)

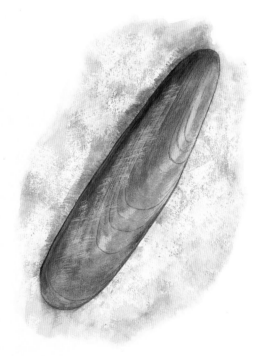

Giant Date Mussel

Family: Mytilidae
Subfamily: Lithophaginae
Size: 11.5cm (4½ in)
Habitat: Coral reefs, boring into soft coral rock in the shallow sublittoral zone to depths of about 40m (130 ft)
Distribution: Southern Florida, the West Indies to the Gulf of Mexico
Importance: Date Mussels are active borers causing significant damage to limestone and concrete structures
Description: A moderately large, elongated, thin shell; its height is about one quarter of the shell length. The outline is narrowly elliptical. A thin dull orange to brownish periostracum covers the white shell. It is sculptured by fine closely spaced vertical striations which cross the fairly distinct growth increments below and defining a line from the umbones to the posterior ventral margin.

The inside of the shell is grey to lilac or white; the muscle scars are usually indistinct: the posterior is roughly half-moon shaped and substantially larger than the circular anterior scar, to which it is joined by a weak pallial line. The hinge line is long and slightly curved with the ligament situated in a narrow groove.

Their common name is derived from their resemblance to a date; the scientific (Latin) name of this genus means 'stone-eater', from their habit of boring into rock. This is achieved by the use of a chemical secretion which dissolves the rock enabling the animal to excavate its hole by twisting the shell around as it bores.

Date Mussels are distributed around the world, mainly in warm temperate to tropical seas. They may bore into relatively soft rock, live or dead coral colonies and thicker shells of other molluscs.

Petricolaria pholadiformis

(Lamarck, 1818)

Family: Petricolidae
Size: 6cm (2¼ in)
Habitat: Rocky shores, low intertidal to sublittoral zone, boring into soft rock
Distribution: North Atlantic, from the Gulf of St. Lawrence to Florida and the Gulf of Mexico; introduced into northern Europe from Norway to West Africa and the Mediterranean; also Pacific coast of North America from Washington to California
Description: This is also known as the American Piddock. The shell is elongated and elliptical with both ends gently rounded. The valves are equally inflated with the umbones in the front quarter of the shell length. The shell is thin, brittle and coloured white. It is coarsely sculptured on the anterior third with 9–12 radial ribs crossed by raised growth lines to produce scales. Posteriorly there are numerous finer ribs becoming obsolete towards the back end.

The inside of the shell is white and the muscle scar impressions weak. The adductor scars are subequal in size and situated near the dorsal margin. The pallial sinus is deep and U-shaped reaching at least half the shell length. The hinge is narrow and characterized by three prominent thin cardinal teeth in the left valve and two in the right valve. The siphons are long and separate in this species.

The False Angel Wing or American Piddock is an increasingly widespread species found boring into soft rock such as clay, chalk, stiff mud and peat. It bores by rotating its rasp-like shell and mechanically grinding into the soft rock. It was introduced into Europe about 100 years ago with the American Oyster (*Crassostrea virginica* Gmelin, 1791).

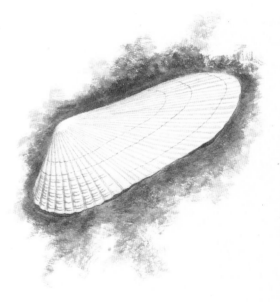

False Angel Wing

GAPER

Arenomya arenaria

(Linnaeus, 1758)

Sand Gaper

Family: Myidae
Size: 15cm (6 in)
Habitat: Sandy shores, low intertidal to sublittoral zone, burrowing to depths of three times its shell length in muddy sand to sandy gravel
Distribution: North Atlantic, from northern Norway to the Bay of Biscay in the east and from the Gulf of St. Lawrence to North Carolina in the west; also in the Pacific Northwest, reported from Alaska to northern California
Importance: A popular food species in Eastern North America where it is marketed under several names
Description: The shell of the Sand Gaper or Soft Shelled Clam is solid, brittle and creamy to chalky white. It is subelliptical in outline, the front end broadly rounded and the posterior end attenuated. The shell is moderately inflated with umbones in the centre. The surface is smooth, lined only by the growth increments. It is covered when young by a buff-coloured periostracum, usually worn from older specimens. The shell gapes at both ends.

Internally the muscle scars are large, subequal in size and joined by a pallial line with a relatively deep U-shaped sinus reaching nearly to the midline. The hinge is without teeth, but the two valves are held together by the strong internal ligament which is situated between the projecting spoon-shaped chondrophore of the left valve and corresponding recess in the umbonal cavity of the right valve. Externally the valves are joined along the posterior dorsal margin by fused periostracum which extends over the very long fused siphons.

The Sand Gaper is known by a number of local names, particularly where it is a popular food species.

GREAT PIDDOCK

Zirfaea crispata

(Linnaeus, 1758)

Family: Pholadidae
Size: 9cm (3½ in)
Habitat: Rocky shores, low intertidal zone to around 75m (246 ft) boring into chalk, clay, stiff mud, peat or wood
Distribution: North Atlantic, from Newfoundland south to New Jersey and from Norway to the Bay of Biscay
Description: This is also known as the Oval Piddock. The medium sized, white shell is subquardate in outline. The front end is obliquely truncated forming a near right angle with the anterior dorsal line. The posterior dorsal line is gently sloping to the round posterior end. The shell surface is distinctly sculptured in two clearly defined areas separated by a smooth median furrow: the anterior is roughly corrugated with 12 radial ribs crossed by raised growth lamellae to form sharp scales; the posterior half is sculptured only by the fine growth lines.

The inside of the shell is distinguished by a single prominent curved tooth-like projection in each valve called the apophysis, to which foot muscles are attached. The pallial line is indented by a broad sinus; the adductor scars are weak. The hinge plate is characterized by a reflected anterior dorsal shield.

The Great Piddock has long fused siphons and a strong muscular foot. Its body is fused ventrally. The shell gapes broadly at both ends and is held together dorsally by a series of accessory plates which may prevent the shell from separating during boring. This species is a mechanical borer. When the larva settles it begins to slowly wear a depression in the rock surface and continues to bore deeper into the substrate as it grows.

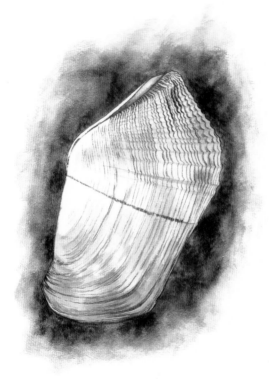

Great Piddock

LUCINE

Codakia orbicularis

(Linnaeus, 1758)

Tiger Lucine

Family: Lucinidae
Size: 9.5cm (3¾ in)
Habitat: Sandy shores, sublittoral zone to depths of around 33m (100 ft) buried in sand or silty sand
Distribution: Southern Florida, West Indies to Brazil
Importance: Used in jewellery and for making decorative ornaments
Description: Also known as the Disc Shell, its shell is moderately large and fairly thick. It is nearly circular in outline and slightly inflated. The colour is usually white on the outside which is distinctly sculptured by numerous curved fine radial ribs crossed by co-marginal cords to give a beaded texture. The surface may be quite shiny.

The interior of the shell is often stained yellow and the hinge plate and margin usually deep to pale coral pink. The beaks are strongly curved anteriorly. The hinge is broad and curved with one prominent anterior lateral tooth, one blade-like cardinal tooth below the beak, a weak posterior lateral behind and the distinct groove of the internal ligament curving inwards. The muscle scars are characteristic for the group, with the elongated anterior scar projecting towards the inner part of the body area connected by an unbroken pallial line to the more quadrate posterior scar.

This species was previously confused with the Indo-Pacific species *Codakia tigrina* (Linnaeus, 1758) with which it is almost certainly closely related; thus the mis-applied common name 'Tiger Lucine'. The more appropriate translation of its valid scientific name is Disc Lucine. The generic name *Codakia* is derived from the Senegalese word for shell, *Codok*.

PACIFIC OYSTER

Crassostrea gigas

(Thunberg, 1793)

Family: Ostreidae
Subfamily: Crassostreinae
Size: 30.5cm (12 in)
Habitat: Sandy to gravelly bays, low intertidal and sublittoral zones, cemented to rocks, gravel or shell fragments
Distribution: Worldwide, but native to southern Japan and South China Sea. Introduced to Pacific Coast of North America, from Alaska to northern California and also north-western Europe (Britain and France)
Importance: Valuable commercially grown food species in Far East, Pacific Northwestern states, Britain and France. Most oysters now marketed in Europe are this species
Description: An elongated irregularly spatula-shaped shell which is relatively lightweight for its size, the Giant Pacific Oyster (also known as the Japanese Oyster) has a thinner shell when grown quickly in relatively warm water of the sub-tropics than in the colder regions. The surface of the shell may be sculptured with 3–4 low rounded radial ribs, interrupted by growth increments which may be produced as flanges caused by the change in direction of the mantle during secretion of the shell. These flanges are thin and usually broken. The shell colour is white with radial streaks of pink to purplish-brown.

The interior is usually chalky white with a single large half-moon shaped muscle scar in the lower, central area, slightly to the posterior side. The hinge line is short and slightly curved; the ligament forms a narrow band along its entire length. The inner and outer ligament layers are clearly defined. The ligamental area is often fairly long.

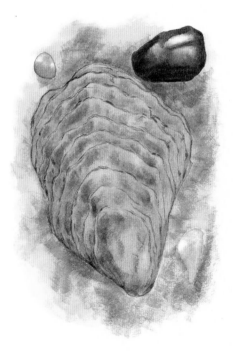

Giant Pacific Oyster

39

PACIFIC RAZOR CLAM

Siliqua patula

(Dixon, 1789)

Family: Cultellidae
Size: 15cm (6 in)
Habitat: Sandy shores, intertidal to sublittoral zone, on exposed coasts
Distribution: Pacific Northwest from Alaska to southern California
Description: The shell is subrectangular in outline with a height-length ratio of about 1:2.5. It is bluntly truncated at the posterior end and rounded at the front. The shell is thin and brittle. The valves are equally inflated and open at both ends. The beaks are in the front quarter; umbones are indistinct. The colour of the shell is grayish-white, covered by a thin shiny, golden brown to greenish periostracum. The surface is smooth, distinguished only by the clear growth stages, defined by dark lines.

The interior of the shell is white and characterized by a distinct broad, low internal rib between the umbonal cavity and the anterior ventral margin of the pallial line. The posterior U-shaped sinus is moderately deep, reaching not quite half the shell length.

This species is commercially fished along the coasts in the northern part of its range (Alaska to Oregon) where a size restriction of about 11.5cm (4.5 in) is imposed to maintain population stocks.

Pacific Razor Clam

PEN SHELL

Pinna carnea

Gmelin, 1791

Family: Pinnidae
Size: 28cm (11 in)
Habitat: Sandy shores, partially buried in sand, sublittoral zone to around 4m (13 ft)
Distribution: Southern Florida and the Caribbean
Description: A large fan-shaped thin brittle shell, pointed at the anterior end, widening towards the posterior end, which may be broadly curved or nearly straight. The margin is usually irregularly broken. The hinge is long and straight, extending virtually the entire length of the dorsal margin of the shell. The ventral margin is slightly concave towards the front, becoming straighter or very slightly convex posteriorly.

The colour is amber to brownish orange. It has 5–8 low rounded irregular radial ribs, distinguished by fairly large, widely spaced projecting hollow spines. These may prevent the shell from being dislodged from the sediment. The inside of the shell is usually a lighter colour, with the pearly body area separated by a longitudal furrow.

Pen Shells form a small family of about 20 species which are all fairly similar. Most species live subtidally in warm temperate to tropical regions, partially buried in clean sand with the pointed front end downwards. The animal attaches its fibrous byssus to small stones or shell fragments beneath the surface.

The long golden byssal threads of the Mediterranean Noble Pen Shell (*Pinna nobilis* Linnaeus, 1758) were used to weave or knit a fabric which has been interpreted as being the legendary 'cloth of gold' of the Middle Ages.

Amber Pen Shell

41

QUAHOG

Mercenaria mercenaria

(Linnaeus, 1758)

Quahog

Family: Veneridae
Size: 11.5cm (4½ in)
Habitat: Sandy shores, intertidal to sublittoral zones to about 16m (50 ft), burrowing near the surface in sand or muddy sand
Distribution: North Atlantic, from Canada to Florida and Gulf of Mexico; introduced into Europe and the Pacific coast (California)
Importance: A valuable food species, exploited since prehistoric times on the east coast; it is eaten either fresh or cooked. The shells were used to make 'wampum' beads.
Description: Also known as the Hard Shelled Clam, the outline of the shell is subtriangular, rounded with high moderately inflated umbones and anteriorly curving beak. There is a well defined, heart-shaped lunule below the beaks and broadly rounded front end. The posterior end is bluntly pointed. The surface is sculptured by the regular growth lines interrupted by the distinct growth stages. The colour is usually white to yellowish and often stained.

The interior of the shell is white with two large adductor scars connected by a fairly wide pallial line. In some specimens the shell is coloured a distinctive deep purple to indigo in the posterior ventral areas. The hinge is irregularly curved with three prominent cardinal teeth in the right valve and two corresponding teeth in the left valve. The valves are joined by a strong external ligament.

The Quahog takes its common name from the ancient Algonquin Indian name, as this species was introduced to the European settlers over 400 years ago. It is sold under a number of different names depending upon the size of the shells.

SCALLOP

Aequipecten opercularis

(Linnaeus, 1758)

Family: Pectinidae
Size: 9cm (3½ in)
Habitat: Off shore, on coarse sand to gravelly sediments, in the sublittoral zone
Distribution: Northeast Atlantic from northern Norway to the Mediterranean
Importance: A commercially important food species trawled from shallow coastal waters in northern Britain and northwards
Description: A medium-sized, moderately inflated shell, nearly circular in outline. It has a short straight dorsal hinge line, characterized by 'ears' either side of the central beaks. The anterior ear is somewhat longer than the posterior and distinguished by a byssal notch. This notch is more distinct on the right valve than the left.

The shell is sculptured with 18–22 strong radial ribs, crossed by numerous raised, fine growth lines. The colour is variable, but mainly in shades of pink to reddish-purple, occasionally yellow or brown; either uniformly or mottled in roughly co-marginal patterns. One colour variety has deep purple ribs on a virtually white shell; it was once considered to be a distinct species.

The Scallops are one of the largest families of bivalves with several hundred species. They are distributed worldwide from cold Arctic and Antarctic seas to the tropics and are found in the intertidal zone to great depths. The Queen and Great Scallop (*Pecten maximus* Linnaeus, 1758) are two important commercial species in Britain. The Atlantic Bay Scallop (*Argopecten irradians* Lamarck, 1819) is the equivalent commercial species of the east coast of North America.

Queen Scallop

SURF CLAM

Hemimactra solidissima

(Dillwyn, 1817)

Atlantic Surf Clam

Family: Mactridae
Size: 23cm (9 in)
Habitat: Sandy shores, sublittoral zone to about 46 m (150 ft); shallow burrowing in muddy sand to gravel often in high energy environments
Distribution: East coast of North America from Nova Scotia to North Carolina
Importance: This species is dredged commercially from New Jersey south to Virginia, and is used for a variety of shellfish dishes, particularly chowder
Description: Often a large fairly thick shell, typically around 18cm (7 in) but may grow larger. It is oval to broadly subtriangular in outline with umbones central and moderately inflated. The surface is marked by the fine growth lines and bands marking major growth stages. The shell is white covered with a thin tan periostracum which is usually eroded from the umbonal area and much of the body of the shell. The posterior area is defined by a weak ridge forming an angle of about 20° with the posterior dorsal margin.

The inside of the shell is marked by the large, subequal, pear-shaped, adductor muscle scars joined by the pallial line which is indented by a distinct U-shaped posterior sinus, extending to about one third of the shell length. The hinge is narrow, characterized by the central triangular pit of the internal ligament, either side of which are a couple of thin cardinals and flanked by a pair of elongated blade-like lateral teeth.

The Atlantic Surf Clam is a fairly typical example of this family of over 100 species which may be found from the tropics to the cold temperate regions.

THORNY OYSTER

Spondylus princeps

Broderip, 1833

Family: Spondylidae
Size: 12.7cm (5 in)
Habitat: Offshore, in the sublittoral zone attached to rocks to a depth of around 33m (110 ft)
Distribution: Pacific coast of North and Central America from Baja California to Panama
Description: A large, heavy, moderately inflated scallop-like shell; the top (left) valve is strongly sculptured with 6–8 strong ribs bearing prominent spines up to 4cm (1½ in) in length. They are either narrow and rolled or spatulate, projecting from a low angle to the shell surface or nearly vertical. In between the primary ribs are 4–5 secondary ribs with shorter, usually narrow, spines. The colour varies from virtually all white with only weak pinkish staining near the umbonal region or white with pinkish-purple stained patches, ribs and spines to more uniformly dark reddish purple.

The hinge line is straight, heavy and characterized by the typical central, triangular ligament set in a depression between two prominent knob-like teeth in the lower (right) valve, which lock into corresponding sockets in the top valve. In this species the ligamental area is distinctly elongated.

The Thorny Oysters are a small family of a single genus including around 40 species. They are all relatively thick shelled with radial ribs bearing spines. The surface of most species is usually encrusted by epiphytes: algae and cementing organisms like worm tubes, bryozoans and spat of other cementing species. Thicker shelled species are also bored by sponges, worms or other molluscs.

Pacific Thorny Oyster

WING OYSTER

Pteria colymbus

Röding, 1798

Grebe's Wing or Wing Oyster

46

Family: Pteriidae
Size: 9cm (3½ in)
Habitat: Rocky shores, subtidally to about 33m (100 ft)
Distribution: North Carolina, southeastern Florida to Brazil
Description: This is also known as the Atlantic Wing Oyster. Its shell is thin, fragile and broadly D-shaped in outline. The hinge line is long and straight from the short wedge-shaped anterior 'ear' to the end of the long narrow posterior 'wing'. There is a short distinct byssal notch just below the anterior ear. The left valve is more greatly inflated than the right valve. The colour varies from golden orange to purplish-brown with lighter coloured narrow broken radial lines. The periostracum is thickened by overlapping, radially arranged, flattened scales.

The interior of the shell is pearly with the body area clearly defined by a wide shiny brown to purple border. The single muscle scar is kidney-shaped and centrally situated. The valves are joined by a long simple ligament; the hinge is essentially without teeth.

The Wing Oysters live attached by a byssus to other marine organisms such as Sea Fans (Gorgonians) and Sea Whips (Antipatharians). They align their posterior wing upwards with the rounded ventral margin of the shell facing outwards to take advantage of nutrient-rich currents.

Wing Oysters are not true 'Pearl Oysters' (genus *Pinctada*), to which they are related. However, the shell of the larger species may be used to make buttons and other decorative objects which are cut from the Mother-of-Pearl inner shell layer.